Lessons
From My Father

100 Pivotal Life Guiding Practices in a
RESOURCE GUIDE

To Benefit Every Child

By Tariq T. Raheem M.A.

Mr. Isaiah Raheem (My Dad) on a motorized scaffold giving instructions to the crew and smiling for the camera.

Lessons From My Father

Printed in the USA

ISBN 978-1-105-40950-9

Table of Contents:

Mr. Isaiah Raheem in the early twenties.

About my father:

My Father, ISAIAH RAHEEM, one of the smartest men I know, is a U.S. Army Vietnam Era Veteran who was born in Mobile, Alabama also known as the "Port City". It is important to know that, life's opportunities were often shortchanged for many African-Americans, but my dad and his dad did not allow it. My father was born in a Colored Persons hospital not much bigger than a living room. His father, like many immigrants in America sought life, liberty, and the quest of better opportunities so he migrated the family to Pittsburgh, Pennsylvania a.k.a. "the Steel City". Many African-American families migrated to avoid lynchings and other Jim Crow practices that would go unpunished in the South, or were the law of the land. After serving in the military with honor as a head cook in Germany, my father settled in another famous port city, Newark, NJ also known as "Brick City".

Surely my dad wanted the best for his seven children, so he did whatever jobs he could get in order to "make ends meet", even if it wasn't cooking. On his quest to interpret the big picture of what is going on in life, he made a huge transformation by becoming a Muslim, and he never used the religion as a tool to divide us from people that exercised other faiths. He was a bibliophile without a college degree, and he never used his knowledge except to lift up his people. Also he emphasized that the color of the other person's skin will not change his commitment to telling the truth as HE saw it, and I, as his son, was fortunate to witness this phenomena.

As the oldest child, I had the burden (now I see as a blessing) to hear all of the lectures, and strategic rants that sometimes would last for hours on a every topic under the sun as my father blew cigarette smoke out the attic window. I learned more about life and people, on the steps of my attic listening to my father, than in any part of my K-12 education. He planted the seeds in my mind, and as I write this I am able to reflect on many more lessons than those enclosed in this book. It is no accident, that I was called "professor" in high school; nor is it an accident that more than half of my siblings are currently educators, perhaps it was one of the goals of my father.

My dad, Isaiah, (top right) is with some of his brothers and sisters.

The Goals of This Resource Guide:

This book is loaded with great life lessons that the reader can read in its entirety, or pick at random a particular area of concern. Famous people, of the past and the present, are sprinkled throughout the book as a source of inspiration, and to verify the significance of the lessons.

The sad reality is that, many children grow up missing some of these healthy guiding rules, and therefore they may have their full potential shortchanged. Statistics show a decline in two-parent homes that consist of a mother and father. Many children are living with a single parent, often the mother. More significantly, because of the economic, social and cultural pressures born upon parents and schools in today's fast-paced challenging world, too often children slip through the cracks. Children wind up missing critical skills and thinking processes that I was lucky to get from both my mother and father.

Perhaps a father, mother, family counselor, or educator could make a positive impact on one life, by discussing just one lesson contained in this book to a child. I am a firm believer that all children need to have a father and mother, in their lives, or at the very least, the lessons and love that may come from such a valuable human relationships.

There is no question that my mother Nadirah Raheem-Nazaha was instrumental in crafting my development, however this book focuses my father, Isaiah Raheem. The seeds of wisdom were planted in my mind as I grew up under the wings of my father. I owe my successes to my dad, the smartest man I know. He made every effort to share his knowledge with me.

Sometimes I didn't follow the advice, and paid the price with unnecessary life experiences. I thought at one point that I could be giving him too much credit, but as I thought about it, I could not synthesize or create new lessons if the seeds of the basic ones were never planted.

Thanks Dad and Mom!!! I also know that I would not have had the creative synthesis of free-thought to draft a book without the support of my loving wife, Stacy Raheem. I finally, must thank God for blessing me to complete this book. May this book, help every child be more successful in life.

Tariq Raheem, and wife- Stacy Raheem at a cousin's wedding reception.

How to use this Resource Guide:

The main contents of the guide: is structured to benefit the needs of **Educators & Coaches, Parents & Adult Relatives of Children, Social Workers, and the Leisure Reader**.

Educators and coaches can teach any topic by using it as a point of discussion, during class or practice. This is easy because, the topics are alphabetically organized by their theme in the Table of Contents. To extract specific meanings from each lesson, they can refer to my analysis and the supporting examples I present. Even if, educators disagree with the experiences I present, there is still an opportunity to raise the issues in the lesson in a different way, for the betterment of the child.   This resource guide will make a great gift for the concerned parent looking for ideas to discuss with their children.

Parents/ guardians and older relatives are advised to pick a lesson from the Alphabetical Table of Content, read my supporting ideas, and then start a discussion with the child about the lesson, but making sure the example I present to support the lesson is shared before moving on to the next lesson. Every now and then, you can present the same lesson to the child, by adding some of your own supporting examples. There are hundreds of different examples to support each lesson.

Social Workers and counselors may want to share some of the lessons raised, in this resource guide, to the families and children they provide services to. Just select a lesson to highlight, and as you share the examples within the lesson you also can encourage the participants to contribute their feelings about the lesson.

Thematic Lessons Listed in Alphabetical Order

Thematic Lessons Listed in Alphabetical Order

Thematic Lessons Listed in Alphabetical Order

Thematic Lessons Listed in Alphabetical Order

1. Accentuate the positive not the negative.

Dwelling on the negative attributes of the child by yelling at him/her, retards the development of the child's positive attributes. If we put too much focus on the bad issues and mistakes made by those around us, then we don't give an opportunity for the good to shine. Everyone can bring something to the table.

As a seven year old boy on a construction site full of my dad's men, I thought I was useless for doing any good work. I was too small to carry a full pan of "mud", (joint compound) that was used by drywall specialists. This did not deter my dad from finding something that I could do. Dad saw the positive, and gave me just a little mud on a spackle knife plus a hammer to make the nail spots smooth on the walls. Eventually, I grew to do more.

If we look for the positive attributes in the child, and encourage them to use those attributes, the child will be better off.

2. <u>Appreciate the gifts you got.</u>

Millions of people go to their graves never making a genuine effort to do what they are really good at it. Usually this occurs because the individual never did an inventory of what they are blessed with. Nothing is worse than to be at the funeral of a young man, and to know he never had a chance to express his gifts, even though he was in an environment where he could have expressed them. If you have life and health, that is a great start. If you have someone who loves you, that's a plus too. When people seem to have so many good things operating in their favor like wealth, friends, and more, they can still feel lost. Suicide rates are alarmingly high in the USA even though there is so much that we can appreciate. When feeling overwhelmed, useless, hopeless, or bullied slowdown and make a list of the qualities, things and people you have in your corner, and if necessary get some help. Make sure your child understands this.

3. Age should not be a barrier to achievement.

Sometimes, employers look at the age of a potential employee, and then use it as a reason to deny employment. Also, we consent to social norms of what age is too young to start a business, or too old to start a new career.

My father would hire people twice his age, even in their seventies, when they can demonstrate aptitude to get the job done. From what I seen, oftentimes these men were more proficient and effective than the younger guys. Additionally, my dad encouraged me to follow my entrepreneurial ambitions. I started a landscaping business, before I was old enough to drive an automobile.

There are countless stories of people that do seemingly uncommon achievements for their age, share this with your child, or the student.

4. **Ask for what you want in life, if you want a shot at getting it.**

Sadly, the culture of society, particularly in the USA, is not generous. Jobs are not just given to you. The bride to be, is not going to say, "I do", without you asking for her hand in marriage. "Ask and you shall receive", is a good first step. Many times my father would drive up on the job and ask for work. This was the only way we got any decent paying jobs. But beyond this, it is also important to ask the right person. If you ask the first person you see on the jobsite, you are probably setting yourself up for failure. You got to ask the decision maker. Never consider yourself accomplished at this task, if the only person you asked, does not have the power to say yes to your question.

If you don't ask, then you certainly are not in the game to get what you want out of life.

5. Be wary of unsolicited compliments.

I love compliments just as well as the next man. *""Nice hair",* *"Nice dress", "Hey, you do that pretty good", "you should run for president",* keep the compliments coming. It feels good, and genuine ones are encouraged.

However, my father thought that when compliments are given to you, they often wind up resulting in negative outcomes. First, flattery compliments can 'swell your head' in other words make you feel that you are better than others, and/ or distract you from your task at hand. Plus, compliments are used, by some, to steer your thinking process into another hidden agenda, or to lull you into complacency and satisfaction with your current situation. This also depends on who it is coming from; boss, friend, family, or stranger.

When you hear compliments, accept them courteously, but know what they may be worth to you.

6. <u>Break the barriers you were not expected to break.</u>

People in general tend to formulate expectations and limitations of your worth, based on a wide range, or a small set of factors. You can be satisfied with this classification of yourself and skip this lesson, but if you want more, then you have to prove yourself.

How many times have different groups been told that they can't do, or should not do a particular job or career? Too many times women and African-Americans have been excluded from positions based on rationalization generated by individuals who may have an agenda that you are unaware of. These individuals are dream killers, and you got to create a new approach contrary to their barrier to your reach your goal. New pioneers are emerging every day. Like **Sonia Sotomayor**, the first Hispanic Supreme Court Justice, they are succeeding at breaking the "glass ceiling'". We are waiting on you.

7. Bring Your Child to the regular external experiences.

Children need to see what you do, and how you do it, if they are going to learn how to do it. How can your child deal with adult experiences properly if you are constantly leaving them at home, in the car, or letting them tune out your interactions with headphones and ear plugs? They can't.

When I was very young, my father would take me in to the various banks where he made deposits or cashed checks for the construction work the crew did. I was able to see how the banks had policies that were more relaxed and friendly in white communities, but if we were doing the same transactions at banks in the black neighborhoods we would get resistance. I was able to watch my father hold them to the same standards. If I wasn't made to come in **and** to observe the patterns at the banks, then I am sure I would have been an easier target to the predatory lending and unfair policies that exist in our communities to this day.

8. <u>Brother by Color does not mean Brother by Spirit.</u>

No race or ethnic group has a monopoly on the crimes occurring across the country. This is true in politics, in business, and on the streets.

After my father dealt with the racism expressed by some owners, builders and contractors, he had to deal with some of his employees. The *"so called brothers"* that were stealing company time and doing other things that undermined the success of his company when he was conducting business away. My dad would remind me that even the person that looks like you will *"stab you in the back"*.

The moral of this story is that, we can't assume that someone has our spirit and values, just because they may look like us. An environment that allows someone to operate in it, that does not share the same code of ethics as all players will be a playground for corruption. Look at the problems plaguing Wall Street, and the unbelievable loss of stocks by investors.

9. CAN'T or "I can't" must be removed from your vocabulary.

When the world is against you, can't is a word you can't afford to use.

When being offered jobs in multi-million dollar homes with 20 foot cathedral ceilings, saying *"we can't do that"*, was not an option for my dad. He would subcontract with people that could get the sheetrock in the ceiling and then get the job done.

Too often when young people don't want to do something or think they are unable to do it, they will cry, *"I can't"*. Parents and educators, we should challenge this statement and push children to do and be more. Everyone can recall an experience where we doubted our ability to complete the task. Share it with them, and push them to do and be more.

10. <u>Clean up after yourself.</u>

When we are in a workplace, school, or home common area, if we cleaned up after ourselves, we would be better off. It could be unsanitary, costly, and hazardous to leave it otherwise. Sometimes we need to be reminded.

Part of the challenge my father faced, on the construction site, was the boss's perception of his crew's work quality. Workers that left big blotches of "mud", (joint compound) that fell off the spackle knife onto the floor made the drywall work look sloppy. The same large blobs of mud also showed a level of wastefulness of construction material that was unacceptable for my father and the owners.

Also, eager customers looking to take an early peak preview of their product, the house, run the risk of slipping and falling on the messy blobs of "mud" left behind by careless workers. And when the blobs of "mud" get hard and dry, it makes the job harder for the wood trimmers, the flooring men, and the clean-up crew working in the area, after us.

The message to the children: It always looks better to clean up after ourselves. Put the Lego blocks away before moving to the next set of toys, and definitely before going to bed.

My father on the job, posing for the camera.

11. <u>Clichés sound good, but be careful when you hear them.</u>

Clichés sound nice, and are general statements that have common truths to them which can be applied to many scenarios. The problem occurs when they are taken out of context, and are meaningless to your situation, or are said only to make you conform to the speaker's way of thinking.

My dad was told on several occasions to, **"Love America or Leave it"**, a popular cliché, we heard, after dad shared a constructive critique of the inequalities that existed in pay and/or treatment on the jobs in American society. They would even sometimes add on to this cliché, **"Go back to Africa"**. My dad's cool response usually got the people promoting the clichés to concede. He reasoned that he had a right to love America and to criticize it, just as we have a right to criticize our children if we want them to do better.

In other words, don't just nod your head to the cliché because it sound nice, no matter **who** it comes from.

12. Chores build character and aptitude.

Chores are the regular errands around the house that children would rather avoid, if given the opportunity. Sometimes parents attach incentives or allowances to the chore, but this is not necessary. The skills acquired during these activities, stay with the child for life.

It is a shame to see young men, that don't have the aptitude to help their mothers or grandmothers with house chores, cooking cleaning, laundry, lawn care, garbage removal, etc.... Growing up, we had to do all of this. The skills I learned doing these chores were transformative, allowing me to quickly adapt to any situation requiring the moving of furniture and the repair of small things around the house.

When I do work at volunteer functions, I am ready to jump in because of the comfort I had to have in completing the odd jobs around the house. Some parents call chores punishment. I call it conditioning for life. Encourage every child to have multiple chores, it builds competency.

13. <u>Collect your debts.</u>

When an organization or a friend owes you money for a job done, it is important to collect the debt, as reasonably and as quickly as possible. The rationale is obvious, but it is easy to let a debt be delayed if it is just owed to you.

My father could not let the debts owed to the company slide or be delayed. Too much was at stake. Many times upon the satisfactory completion of a job my father had to work diligently to secure payment. Sometimes, the contractors would seem to get amnesia on Friday and not show up to make payment for completed work, causing the entire staff to go home without pay. To prevent this, my dad had to collect early, or structure payroll in such a way that it was not the same day as his payday.

If you are owed money, do your best to see to it that it is paid when the work is completed. The longer you wait, the harder it is to collect payment.

14. Command Respect from all comers.

Respect should be given by all. Sometimes it has to be earned. And some people expect you to demand your respect. I think what most people want is, courtesy and civility when they are interacting with others.

Every now and then, employees of my father would get the impression that they could talk to him as if they were talking to an animal in the street. This would be a mistake and he would correct them just by changing the tone of voice. If there was a boss talking to my dad, in a tone that he felt was less than **'man-to-man respect'**, my father would immediately let him know of the violation and remind him that he is talking to a man just like him. It usually ended with the boss blushing and apologizing to him.

Don't let people talk to you any kind of way, and don't curse at your child. This behavior sets the child up to accept this type of abuse as an adult; and does not prepare her to deal with the professional adult world.

15. <u>Computers will be the future get use to it.</u>

Many careers in the 21st Century require workers to be computer literate. If you can't do the basics of Microsoft Office system interactions, you may become obsolete.

About thirty-two years ago, my father predicted the need for me to be computer literate. I don't know how he knew. So he purchased a Commodore VIC 20 and the 64 model for us to work on. He ordered us not to play games on it. He said, "It's for learning." That didn't work too well, because I played a lot of games in the name of learning. What did work pretty well was his request for me to get specialized training at the middle school early in the mornings.

Listening to my father, on this lesson, gave me the extra computer training that helped me to feel comfortable with all of the technological innovations that eventually came in the Twenty-First Century.

16. Common Sense should not be uncommon.

When human beings collect information about the environment and society via one/ or more of their five senses, (sight, hearing, smelling, taste, and touch) the brain then processes that information for practical use. Common sense is the designation given to the individual that demonstrates effective management and utilization of the information presented in the environment.

On a daily basis we see that when common sense is not utilized the individual failing to use it suffers the consequences. My experience in seeing it on the job is when, someone spends more time trying to avoid work by hiding in the closet or other tricks, and it seems like they are working harder at avoiding work than if they would just complete the task at hand. There is something wrong with this type of thinking; it does not show common sense.

Common sense is missing when people in government fail to advocate for programs that benefit their constituents, or they support a program that might has irreparable harm on the social fiber of the community.

Common sense has also failed all of us in economic policies. Think about all of the financial burdens brought upon small businesses that were required to enforce the **Plessy v. Ferguson Decision.** They had to create two separate facilities for white and colored people. Think about the social harms they were upholding. Now just think; how much common sense is there to continue to hold on to these old Jim Crow ways of thinking. Legal Jim Crow, is suppose to be dead, but there are some people that are still holding onto ideologies that make no sense.

Let us encourage our children to make decisions that use common sense, so that we don't repeat the mistakes of those before us.

17. <u>Constructive Criticism for those we love most.</u>

Critiques with the mission of improving the condition of an individual done with respect, candor and care, can go a long way to save the loved one from embarrassment in a public school or work venue.

Sometimes when we give a critique to love ones, the critique feels like a rebuking of the person and not the act. We must be careful here. On the same token the loved one receiving the constructive criticism must have a humbly spirit to absorb the advice. I am not saying to *candy coat* the issue, but if you are dealing with people (including family) you have to build the relationship before you take a posture that is uncomfortable for the other.

How, where, and when you offer a critique will determine the effectiveness of the discussion. Put some thought behind it. Yelling or embarrassing a child in public for a behavior you have accepted for a long time might make success in this effort more futile.

18. <u>Consult family and experts if you need help.</u>

This lesson is a continuation of the last one. If you as a parent or educator are not getting through to the child or student, there is nothing wrong with seeking help.

Maybe the child sees something in your character that impedes on his/ her ability to be receptive to your perspectives. Maybe we have to develop different approaches. As the parent/ adult you have an obligation to do everything reasonable in your power to reach the child, even if it means seeking outside help to get the job done.

The child might not thank you now, but hopefully the child will appreciate your efforts down the road.

19. Courage is…

Courage is standing up for what you believe, even in the worst of circumstances.

The first thought that came to my mind was the heroic courage exuded by **Reverend Dr. Martin Luther King Jr**. This is a man that even under the most wicked of treatment, by government sanctioned thugs, remained committed to the non-violent tactics. These tactics were trademarks of **Mahatma Gandhi's** movement in India. Also if we look at the actions of **El-Hajj Malik El-Shabazz**, we notice a similar pattern. To advance the cause of Al-Islam as a religion of peace for black people, **Mr. Shabazz**, also known as **Malcolm X**, combated more racism and social problems with his words and debate than most men, then or now.

Teach the children to establish principles to stand firm on, and then teach them to have the courage to stick with those principles, as long as they believe they are correct.

20. <u>Crazy but right, how is that possible?</u>

When people call someone crazy, it is usually became the person does something out of the normal way people do something. That much is true. The other idea that runs parallel to calling someone crazy is that they are wrong, or that I wish I had the nerve to do what they did, or to say what they said.

Regarding my father, I heard people call him crazy, even the bosses. If they are sincerely listening to him though, they will almost say simultaneously, **"You are crazy, but you are right."** Real leaders appreciate someone that challenges their normal way of thinking, because it gives them an opportunity to improve their business. Dad would get the construction jobs that were not earmarked for him. He recruited men that were not necessarily wanted by other contractors and train them so that they could get the job done, and he was crazy enough to give then a decent salary.

That's the type of crazy that is admirable.

21. Create a job.

If there are no jobs hiring in your profession, some people go back to school to switch careers, others sulk and say why me or poor me.

However, where I come from, we were taught the concept of **"Do For Yourself"**. This principle says that we must be men and women that take the responsibility of raising our family, and if that means creating a job by selling newspapers or other products that people can use in our community then this is what we must do.

Entrepreneurs are constantly creating jobs for themselves and others, as they craft a service or product that the people need or want. The sky is the limit regarding the potential in this lesson.

22. <u>Dine at the dinner table.</u>

This is one of the best times to bond the family and to instill your values in the child.

Experts say this bonding should occur five times a week. Dinner at the dinner table helps a child to learn proper etiquette when eating, plus you can go over the day's highlights in a relaxed family environment. I try to keep the tradition of prayer before we eat, and to appreciate the little or much that we are blessed with.

Dinner should go uninterrupted by calls, I-pods, television, and all that stuff. You can even get the child involved in the preparation of food before, and the clean up after the meal.

Don't miss this opportunity to bond with the child.

23. <u>Disagreement does not mean we must be disagreeable.</u>

Everyone has seen the scenario of a small child who puts up a tantrum in the supermarket because he can't get what he wants. Some may reason that it is cute because he is a baby.

The problem is though, that the tantrum, does not allow the parent to concentrate on the real task at hand, which is, getting through checkout without buying the candy. The parent has already disagreed with the child, and has made earlier concessions to purchase or do something for the child at a later venue, but the child refuses to stop crying or accept negotiated terms. **The child is now being disagreeable.** The immature child is willing to embarrass the parent, and hold her hostage at the counter until he gets the candy he wants, even though she just spent necessary disposable income on a Transformer toy for him yesterday.

This scenario sounds familiar to you, because you may have seen children perform this routine of, *"no negotiation"*, *"it is my way or no way"*; but you may have also seen adults behaving this way at meetings, etc...

However the most glaring example of adults behaving disagreeably, (like children), could have been the summer of 2011 **Congressional meltdown**, where Congress was willing to stop regular working Americans from getting certain government benefits because they were unwilling to negotiate on a budget plan. And then in the winter of 2011, when there was an impasse by Congress that almost caused a tax hike on Americans that can least afford it.

We can teach our children to do better. If two out of three judges in a debate round vote for the team that one judge disagrees with; the judge in the minority does not stop the tournament because he didn't get what he wanted, he moves on to the next round. So should we.

24. <u>Do the right thing.</u>

One of the greatest gifts to human beings is the ability to make choices. The decisions we make daily impact our personal lives and the lives of those around us.

I remember a time when my father could not collect on one of the jobs that his crew completed. He could have lost his composure and ended up in jail, but he made the decision to walk away before something worse happens.

By the way, he still paid his workers, because he knew that they had families to manage. He did what he had to do, to survive and take care of the business.

The moral of the story is, that we all will be confronted with tough issues, but it is not the situation that makes the person, but it is how we deal with it that determines our greatness. Do the right thing.

25. <u>Don't become angry.</u>

Anger is only one letter away from danger. If all participants in a conflict become angry, it can result in violence and nothing is accomplished. This is a major test for many of us in our daily interactions.

Jackie Robinson, the African-American baseball player that broke the color line of Major League Baseball did pass this test. Baseball fans at stadiums would call him the worst racial slurs you can imagine, and they threw black cats and other debris at him as he stepped on to the baseball field to play the game. They did this for no other reason than they wanted the game of baseball for themselves and other racist motives. If Jackie Robinson became angry and retaliated the consequences would have been terrible.

Take charge of your emotions, don't let others control your attitude and find different ways to channel your energies.

26. Don't co-sign with unfair economic policies.

Sometimes bosses will do almost anything to get a profit. Overcharging certain groups for the same products and services is wrong and unethical.

One insurance company created a rule where they sold a very good life insurance policy to people in white communities. My father learned about it, so he wanted to sell the same product to people in his community, but he was instructed to sell the inferior product and to not offer to sell the better product. He could not support this unfair practice so he stopped working for the company.

Similar policies existed in many industries across America. Here is my thought, based on my father's character. Even if it may cost you financially, try to have the integrity to not support unfair policies for profit.

27. <u>Don't do things because others are doing it.</u>

Peer pressure for the right thing is ok. However if your only answer to doing something is that, "everybody is doing it"; then maybe you should think about it before doing it.

During my high school years, the sheep skin coat was a popular, must have item, by many children, and I wanted to get one too.

My father stopped me from succumbing to the peer pressure; the narrative he gave me, was that the coats were expensive, and the trend might have negative consequences in our urban environment where crime was very high.

He said this just before, the problem was reported that many kids were being robbed, in some cases at gun point, and were being shot over the coat. I had the money to buy one, but it is a good thing I listened. My life is more valuable than the need to sport the coat that my friends have.

The lesson is still relevant for today. People are fighting at shopping malls to get the latest Air Jordan Nike sneaker. Material objects are giving many of our children a false sense of their individual worth. Let's teach our children not to be pressured into material things, and that their life and success is more important.

Typical sheepskin coat

28. <u>Don't drink and drive.</u>

This position sounds obvious, and it is the law. Impaired driving, in just the year 2009, is responsible for 12,744 deaths across the USA; 1,437 of these death in the state of Texas alone. For more statistics, see <u>www.acoholalert.com</u>.

My dad's position was to NOT drink at all.

Just think about how many lives would have been saved, and how many more innocent family member lives would NOT have been irreparably damaged because of this vice.

Drinking intoxicates the mind and is a very expensive and damaging part of our culture and if you can avoid it totally I think we will be better off.

29. Don't smoke around your children.

We are confident that smoking can lead to cancer and increased death rates. We now know; that second-hand smoking also leads to cancer.

Long before the report on the dangers of second-hand smoke, from the **Surgeon General**, about thirty years ago, my father knew that something was wrong with smoking around children so he didn't. He went one step further by discouraging us to not smoke. All of my siblings listened and we don't smoke.

What is scary in today's climate is the subtle marketing of the candy flavored mini-cigars emerging at many neighborhood stores. Some young people perceive these cheaper cigarillos, as a healthier option to the traditional cigarette. This is false, they still cause cancer and other problems associated with tobacco products. Encourage them to do the research.

30. <u>Don't drive and text or talk on the cellphone, take the Oprah pledge.</u>

Oprah Winfrey had it right, cell phone usage while driving can and does lead to increased death rates.

On her Oprah Winfrey Show, she took the strong position of BANNING CELLPHONE USE WHILE BEHIND THE WHEEL. She encouraged every American to sign a pledge agreeing to this commitment.

Usually, I can tell when the driver in front of me is on the phone, they are usually driving slower or erratic because of the distraction. My dad always told me to, *"keep my eyes on the road"*. When I am driving, I know I can't be safe, if I am on the phone or texting.

According to the **National Council of Safety** there will be approximately 1.4 million fewer accidents annually if we committed to the **Oprah Winfrey Cell Phone Pledge**.

31. Don't give up!

Life is about struggle in order to get the things we want and need. Sacrifice is always associated with the struggle.

If the Egyptian people would have given up their efforts to overthrow **President Hosni Mubarak**, the longtime leader of Egypt, we might not have witnessed an Egypt governed by the people.

The **Arab Spring** starting in several African nations might be part of the inspiration behind the **Occupy Movement** spreading across the USA.

As long as you are alive, there is always hope. Align yourself with people that think like you, and with people that have similar spirit. Collectively we can win.

32. <u>Don't wait for others to give you anything.</u>

Businesses and organizations that need your services or products are not going give you the business without effort on your part.

The black men working for my father wondered how my father was able to secure large jobs for companies like **K. Hovnanian, Turner Construction, R& S Strauss, and Rite-Aid.**

From the way I saw it, dad had a confident and aggressive desire that broke the color line. He would drive up to the General Contractor trailer of any jobsite and start to sell what he could do for them.

He had no clubs or organizations that he could flaunt to get him connected. He might be the only black person in the entire town. Rejection happened a lot. And it seemed as if they would always immediately discount and dismiss him because he was black, but he would clearly communicate that we could genuinely get the job done.

This trait of his, kept us in business. Many times we were called back to the jobsite when the owner or builder had time to think about the sales pitch dad gave them. Dad's constant phone calling also helped to secure the jobs we needed.

33. <u>Do what you love while helping people.</u>

It is good to have a job, but if you hate the job, it can wind up being toxic for you and the clients you serve.

If possible, try to find a job or career you enjoy doing.

If you love your job the clients you serve will notice.

And if you hate it they will notice that too.

The probability of effectively helping people more increases when you enjoy what you are doing. Look for ways your current job helps people and then cherish those work experiences.

Finding the career or job you love, makes Monday mornings feel like Saturday mornings. Isn't that wonderful?

34. Dress for the job, and Dress for success.

From Wall Street to Main Street every profession has a dress code. Some may seek to resist following the dress protocol, but this leaves you disconnected from your work force.

Even in the drywall industry, as a finisher, my dad told us to dress wearing the color white. It took me a while to realize the significance of the dress code for us. When I did dress in the uniform color requested by my father, I ended the day, much cleaner looking because the materials we worked with were white in color. With the right attitude, I developed a sense of pride in my dress and greater distinction from other construction workers.

My advice to young people is, **to grow up!** Practically every profession requires a dress code and or uniform, if you are looking for individuality, demonstrate it in the excellence of your work.

35. Double standards destroy the fiber of democracy.

Nothing is worse than having the rules of the game change for you because you are different. In a democratic society, theoretically, we want the best person to do the job. In a society that is plagued with double standards we pick the people we like, even if the other person is more qualified. This practice makes any organization run less effectively; therefore undermining democracy.

If one group is shut out of an opportunity, it leads to another group reaping the benefits from the former group. If the latter group receives unearned benefits from the former group, this will create the environment for the latter to perform less work for the equivalent dollar. Equity and a balanced democracy would best be served if both parties were paid the same amount for the same amount of work.

As a history teacher I teach my students about many forms of double standards existing in America and the world. For years, women were paid less for similar jobs, and were denied promotions to higher positions in many companies across the country. The historic justification for this discrimination was that, *"women don't take care of families, but men do"*. This justification in modern times is baseless, since there are millions of women nationwide raising households without a spouse.

Notwithstanding, the **U.S. Supreme Court ruling** to dismiss a class-action discrimination lawsuit against **Walmart**, I believe we still must challenge double standards by any means lawful. Otherwise the double standards are sure to continue. Hopefully, the women in the new filing against Walmart will have success similar or better than the African-Americans of the **Brown v. Board of Education** decision.

36. Education opens doors.

Education is the great equalizer. **Frederick Douglass** was convinced that as he learned how to read he would be able to break the shackles of slavery off his wrists, and off the wrists of millions of his brethren held in bondage.

What gave my father the advantage over many men in securing large construction jobs, was his ability to read building blueprints. I also learned how to read blueprints under my father's tutelage. Now I could create cost estimates for the drywall construction portion. After this he would send me to the builders to pick up the big initial deposit checks.

I am glad that I paid attention in my algebra, geometry, and reading classes.

37. Engage life, by enjoying the moment and the people with you.

We don't know how long we will live. We could live long lives or it could be rather short. Why wait until a funeral to let the people you know that you appreciate and value them.

I cry a little less, because I know that I did cherish, to the best of my ability, the loved ones and the people I interact with on a regular basis. **My cousin, Pamela Lundy-Saleem,** was a lovely lady that embraced every experience with passion. Her children always got 100% of her motherly love, and amazingly, that same 100% she had for them was shared with my children. She never missed a moment to engage the people around her to do the best they could.

Make sure you are doing all that you can to embrace the moments you have, and perhaps we all will remember the best moments that you brought to the table.

38. <u>Equality is what I work for and hope to achieve.</u>

Some believe that Equality is a utopia (perfect society) and that it, is impossible achieve. Even if I would agree with that theory, I don't think we should just sit back and let things be.

My father also believed that he was entitled to fair pay on the construction site. Sadly, when we did the math with white contractors in the same field, we often found that they were being paid almost double the amount per square foot of sheetrock at some jobs than the black crews. In order to get equal pay, my father had to create some clever methods to circumvent this cruel form of profiteering. And we were the lucky ones. When we worked in the inner-city of Newark, prevailing wages were supposed to be issued to all who worked, but the Mexican workers were paid far-below minimum wage. This was very sad.

Because we knew better, we could not accept this substandard pay. We pushed back, and demanded equality of pay. We also knew that if we did not strive for it, then contractors would pay us even less than the substandard pay we were getting.

We have to work for our fair share in the industry.

39. <u>Excellence is worth striving for.</u>

I believe our mission is to strive, the best we can at any task that we agree to perform.

I learned this lesson from my father. No matter what the pay we received from the jobs we agreed to do, our trademark was to complete the job with excellence. I guess this is why we were able to get jobs all across the state of NJ and going into NY. I remember one day when a lady who owned one of the mansion homes we were working on came in. She carried a yard stick, looking for uneven indentations on the thirty foot long picture wall in her living room. I worried about what she would see, my father did not. He knew that we did the best quality of work. His confidence in this fact, of our producing excellent work, led to us working on numerous multi-million dollar homes.

If you are not striving for excellence you might just be shortchanging yourself.

40. FEAR God Alone.

People are often afraid of people or things that have no real power over their lives. Too often FEAR is conjured up. F.E.A.R. is really False Evidence Appearing Real.

I remember there was an opportunity for me to join a really good academic program that I overheard someone talking to another person about. However, when I asked the person for information, the person was FEARful that I might take his position within the program so he choose not to share with me. In time, my determined spirit and faith guided me to find the same program, and to excel through it.

At the end of the day, we should make a resolve to be fearful of the One. We should be fearful of only God if we are thinking to do wrong to others. The giver of life and death and the governor of all circumstances in between is God. That's where our fear should be.

41. Find a Mentor in your industry.

A good mentor in your industry is an individual that accomplishes three things for you. First, they model the best techniques for you to adopt, in order to do your job well. Secondly, they make your work environment as welcoming as possible so that you can focus on being successful. Finally, they have the intuition to know you are going to grow in the profession, so they allow you to autonomy to exercise your talent and offer constructive criticism for you to build on.

My father had people that would guide him with words of wisdom in his profession, and I was lucky to have an incredible mentor as I was completing my teaching certification, **Mr. Kevin Lennon** a veteran Social Studies teacher. Without Mr. Lennon's excellent modeling and insight, about fifteen years ago, my teaching career might have ended before it started. He was a man that I have grown to honor and respect. To this day, I reflect on, and try to mimic some of the pedagogy he used in his day-to-day work.

If you are a student in school or new on the job, do whatever you can to identify and use a mentor to help you grow, the winner will be you.

Find a mentor to help to grow and learn.

42. <u>Focus on your dream.</u>

Dreams are the thoughts that exhibit your wishes for the future. Without dreams life may seem meaningless.

My dad is a dreamer. I know he wishes for his children to have extreme success, which is why he pushes us so hard. He was determined to see me do the kinds of things that would have influence over many; I guess that's why I am an educator and not a construction worker. He would make this fact clear, when he talked to his bosses. If any contractor boss made the mistake of assuming I was being trained, by dad, to take over the family construction business; the conversation would end with an apology from the boss for insulting my father. Then the boss would give dad the paycheck for a job well done.

It doesn't matter what your dreams are about, until you are doing something to make those dreams a reality.

43. Get back up if you are knocked down.

This is a cliché that is worth embracing. The race is not over, until you decide not to stand up, after you fall.

I knew a person who failed a CDL certification test. He tried again several more times without success. After being knocked down from the test for the last time he was ready to give up and throw in the towel, but something in him, decided to study and try it one more time. He eventually passed that test, and he is thankful that he did not stay down and give up.

If you are knocked down seven times then you better get up eight.

44. <u>Get your share of the pie.</u>

People come from all over the world to America, and when they come here, they only want their fair share of the American pie.

My dad wanted the same things, a family, house, home, and business. He did get a chance to achieve all of this. I aspire to do the same.

I think it is natural for anyone willing to work hard and smart to get their share of the pie. There is plenty of pie to be shared, in the United States of America.

45. <u>Go to where the work is.</u>

Work gives man a sense of worth, I grew up enjoying work.

We could rarely find decent paying construction work in our hometown of Newark, even though there was plenty of new housing being built there. We had to drive about an hour each morning to get work at a decent pay rate, which is why we were often doing drywall work in the large new houses of Bergen County. On construction sites it was also common place to see guys drive up from Alabama, Texas, Virginia and Maryland just to get the opportunity to work.

We were not alone in the struggle, many men traveled far, so that they could take care of their families.

46. <u>Goal Setting Blueprints the Dream.</u>

Fail to plan, then plan to fail. It is a lot harder to make a dream materialize if you don't write it down.

The million dollar homes that were being erected, as we pulled up to the jobsite, always had blueprints. My father would always take a peek at them. Dad knew that doing this would help him to guide his construction crew in the direction of the owner's vision. I learned that if I wanted people to follow my dream, then I better have something tangible for people to follow.

Here is a powerful life changing idea for any older child. Parents or guardians can ask the child to write down a list of five to ten goals they hope to achieve in life. Then have the child put the list in a place that is regularly visible, like on their bedroom door. It will serve as a constant reminder of what they want to achieve. Then the child can discuss steps they can do right now to meet the goal. The goal list will be the child's blueprint for life, and just like an architect, they can make additions and changes to the printed idea.

47. <u>God Is Greater than All Things.</u>

"One nation under God" is repeated by millions of school children daily as they recite the Pledge of Allegiance. "In God We Trust" is inscribed on our money. There is an apparent inclination of reverence to a higher power in our society.

Some may wish not to talk about God. We seem able to talk about everything else but we would rather skip over this topic, except in our most desperate and tragic times. There was a brother whom I was very close to that I shared many of my problems to, his name was Brother Rasheed. I use to wonder why he would say, "God is Greater", for each of the problems I told him about. I finally figured it out, it was really rather simple. God IS GREATER than all our problems and concerns.

48. <u>Hatred from others must not stop our resolve.</u>

When a group is determined to accomplish something, what can stop them? Nothing at all can stop them.

During the times of slavery, in the USA, African-Americans were banned from reading. This was the interpretation of the law that existed. Masters would severely punish slaves that were caught learning how to read. So blacks people would find clever ways to teach each other and learn from others in such a way that their masters could not know. They would hide their reading books in their bosom, in their hats, in their pants. African-Americans would meet late at night in the fields away from the master's house to study. Whatever it took, to learn they cherished the chance to do so.

This powerful resolve to learn by African-Americans continued beyond slavery. The Freedmen's Bureau with the help of black people established over 3,000 schools in the South. The resolve of the newly Freed African-Americans had a major impact on the public school system in areas where schools did not exist for this demographic in America. For more information on this topic search: www.digitalhistory.uh.edu .

49. <u>Honesty with family will help you grow.</u>

In theory and in practice, it is often the family that has the most to gain from YOUR success.

If you have a dilemma that is hard to manage at school or work, sharing it with a key family member like a spouse, father, mother, aunt, uncle, or older sibling is a viable healthy option. One of them may help you to sort through your options, and at the very least serve as a sounding board to help you relieve stress. Consider talking to them about your situation, you might be pleasantly surprised by the results.

Conversely, keeping problems to yourself may lead to added stress and sickness.

50. Hurry to you calling for success.

Your dreams are important for the benefit of yourself and humanity. If you put them on hold or if you are slow to take action, for whatever reason, then it is likely someone else will come along and implement your idea almost exactly as you envisioned it.

Thomas Edison is known for his many electrical inventions, but he is best known for the light bulb and particularly the filament inside the bulb that creates the light. What is not known, is that he was constantly in competition with other electrical inventors to submit patents to the copyright office before the other prolific inventors. There was at least one instance where he beat the competition by just a few hours.

If Thomas Edison had taken a lax posture about implementing his dream, would there be a museum erected in his honor in Essex County NJ?

51. <u>Influence your children while you can.</u>

When children become adults, what you did with them, and for them, as a child might determine how they are engaged with you, when they become adults.

If you did not give them the time of day during their childhood years, how can you expect them to want to do the same when they grow older? You don't have to have money to do it. Spend time with your child on the weekends, take them to the park and play with them, read to them daily, sing songs with them, play board games with them, go to your child's baseball game, take them to the store on a regular basis, or just have conversations about current events, future goals, family, sports or life; every minute you spend teaching them, impacts their success in the future.

If you are not taking charge and having influence on them, then the television, negative music, gangs, the opposite sex (when that time comes) will have an open door to influence them without your input. Parents and caretakers can manage this issue.

52. Ignorant people are your most dangerous types.

An ignorant person either does not know information that can help/ hurt him and others, or the ignorant person knows that something can help or hurt him and others but intentionally chooses NOT to take the most intelligent action.

In fact, an ignorant person is known to make the choice or do the action that has potentially the worst consequences for themselves and those around them.

Unfortunately society is full of examples of ignorant persons here are a few: the angry person, the robber, the burglar, the drunk driver, the driver that can't put down his phone, the drug addict, the pedophile, the racist, the instigator, the agitator, the "crabs in a bucket mentality" and perhaps you can think of other generic names.

An ignorant person goes through great effort to make sense out of what can make absolutely no sense. They will at the same time, try to pull you into the problem. Unless you are in a position to teach or help this person to help this person to get on the right path like a teacher, social worker, police officer, doctor, or judge, the best thing you can do is to stay away from them.

53. Imagination must be utilized.

Imagination is a human gift that is in near infinite supply. The main limitation placed on this tool is **conditioned closed mindedness** of our own actions and those around us.

Teachers and parents can use this idea to frame more creative experiences that will bring out the best in a child. And when a child has the intuition to use imagination to complete a task differently, the engaged parent, teacher or social worker should steer this energy and not necessarily be quick to shut it down. Conversely, the child should not be allowed to just violate established principles without regard because of a perceived need of, not having to do what others do, 'because I am better attitude'. There must be balanced management of imagination to get the most out of it.

Learning the consistent basics about nature and science via the **National Geographic** magazines my mom and dad brought me, helped me to realize that many human inventions are born out of the concepts of nature. Here are a few quick examples: birds gave the birth to the idea of human flight via airplanes; the horse's consistent pace equates to a consistent measure of engine power called horsepower; the Internet is called the world wide WEB because of its similarity to the spider web; and we build houses just as the beaver builds a dam and the bird builds a nest.

Family or school trips to museums are incredible opportunities to build on a child's curiosity and imagination. The **Newark Museum** is visited by people from everywhere, and I believe it is FREE for Newark residents with identification. Take advantage.

54. Inspect what you expect.

If you can see a pattern of issues that slow productivity, then you also can predict what might happen next, and therefore create new inspection procedures to prevent a bad outcome.

There are many real life examples to support this position. My father knew that a few of his men had a problem with *'sticky fingers'*. Employee theft is a problem in almost every organization, so this should not be a surprise to any readers of this book. These men were useful in other ways, but if we had to work in homes where people lived in, these workers were not selected.

Bob Ciasulli, one of the auto sales giants on the East Coast, lived by this cliché for many reasons. New car salesmen that failed to inspect a new car delivery coming out of the prep shop, may find a car that wasn't cleaned properly. This could result in less than fully-satisfied customers, and could impact the money flow for the over twenty dealerships that I believe he owned at that time. **We should inspect whatever is a priority for us.**

55. <u>Intoxicants for the mind must be rejected.</u>

Many of the problems existing in American society are linked to the usage, abuse and/or addiction of illegal drugs, and alcohol. These substances have irreparably damaged millions of lives. Although some say, *"they love the buzz felling it gives them"*, these substances fog the minds of the users so that they are not in full sync with reality.

If used on the job, alcohol and drugs would make a life-saving doctor behave dangerously. Plus these substances can be addictive, and extremely costly to the user. Every now and then, my vehicle is sideswiped by someone that was probably drunk behind the wheel late at night.

We all pay higher car insurance premiums, for the burdens placed on us by those that choose to consume intoxicants.

56. <u>Invest in yourself.</u>

This will make you more marketable in your journey to find a career or acquire a spouse.

Investing in yourself could be as simple as going back to school to get your G.E.D., going back to college for additional training, or attending a technical post-secondary school. The knowledge you gain can't be taken away.

My father made huge investments in his business by purchasing tools and having several vehicles always ready for the transport of men, materials, and tools.

He encouraged the men to by their own spackle knives, stilts, and screw guns.

The most successful workers of his men made the investments so that they could become independent after they were trained.

57. <u>Jeopardizing yourself for a moment of pleasure or rage is NOT cool.</u>

The jail cells are full of people that make this mistake.

To get quick pleasure by something they want but can't afford, a person may do something unethical to get it. There are many examples of this from, **"Main Street to Wall Street"**, where people steal from individuals or businesses.

Also, road rage; is prevalent now more than ever as drivers seek to make other drivers pay for thoughtless driving.

These actions are illegal, so why waste our time by shortchanging your intelligence for a mere moment of satisfaction. If someone cuts in front of me, my assumption is that this individual is sick, or that he really needs to have the moment, or else he will have a bad day.

I would try not to get upset, just let it go and keep it moving.

58. Keep healthy relationships active.

Healthy relationships with family members, significant others, and with people in the workplace or church is an important part of our health and wellness. Health can be driven by our social interactions.

My father and mother made it their business to make sure that I knew my cousins, aunts and uncles, by planning trips to see them as often as financially possible. My childhood was enriched for the better, from these experiences.

59. <u>Knowledge similar to food; should be shared.</u>

You may have heard the expression, **"food for thought"**, it applies to this lesson. Knowledge is like food for the mind. When someone knows something that could help a situation and it is suppressed, it is like entering a room full of hungry people, with your lunch, but not offering to share.

Nothing was more disturbing, to my father, than to have someone mislead him because they did not disclose acquired knowledge that may impact him. It did not matter if that person was the boss, his employees, or family. It would hurt him just as much.

Not sharing gathered intelligence between governmental agencies is suggested as one of the precursor issues leading to the September 11th, 2011 attacks on the World Trade Center. This was a sad day in our history. To prevent this from happening again and to get more citizens involved in the prevention of terrorism authorities are reminding us that, "if we see something, say something".

60. Less than perfect, it's OK.

If perfection is the criteria for selecting our leaders then we might not select any.

My father built his business by hiring guys that were not hired by others. They were less than perfect, but he gave them very decent salaries based on their training performance.

This opportunity gave those men a second chance to get their lives back on track and helped them to take care of their families. It was also a vehicle to prevent the recidivism rate in Newark, because he hired them right off the street.

61. <u>Live within your means.</u>

You don't have to keep up with and purchase the latest products and styles marketed on television, and radio commercials.

There is a lot of needless pressure that we face, daily, when we buy expensive products that we can't afford. Too many families across America struggle to live within a fixed budget. Contrary to this marketers try to promote their products. They want to convince you that your life is incomplete without their product. Do I really need to have that twenty dollar automatic egg slicer? I can cut the eggs myself just as fast. Do I really need another pair of hot snuggly slippers, when my daughter doesn't wear the ones she got? Do I really have to purchase the latest plasma HD 3D 4G television built into my cellphone with a "rule the air" unlimited hotspot? How much is that going to extract from my monthly fixed budget? More than I can afford.

"No, we can't buy that product, because truthfully we can't afford it." This is what it means, to live within your means.

62. Mentoring others will help you.

Mentoring is a task that not only a helps the student being mentored to grow, but it also is a transformative process for the person that is mentoring.

How do we know? Some of the most remarkable students, educators, coaches and parents I know are the ones that have consistently mentored/ taught others to be better at a given task. These individuals have proven their value as humans and have demonstrated the highest level of mastery of a concept just because they were able to effectively teach and share the concept for the genuine benefit of the person being mentored.

My top debaters were the ones that readily accepted this role of peer-to-peer teaching. If you are sharing any of the concepts in this book to a child or another adult, then you too are enjoying a transformative process that only mentors and teachers have.

63. <u>Mind over Matter.</u>

The cliché question, *"What is the matter, with you?"*, undermines the value of the mind. Placing matter/ material and body, over the mind.

My father would ask the question differently. He would ask, *"What's on your mind?"*, this showed the high value he placed on what you were thinking about. He knew that it was your thoughts that really determined your wellness, and that your thoughts should be looked upon as the governing factor.

Hopefully we can begin to raise questions that appeal to the mental aspiration of our children. Abolitionist **Sojourner Truth** once said, "It is the mind that makes the body."

64. Nature and Outdoors can help you relax.

The positive impact a trip to the zoo can have on a child is immeasurable.

My father loved taking us to the Delaware Water Gap, and as a young boy I loved it too. I still can remember the exertion I needed to make it halfway across the river. I remember inflating large truck inner tubes that we used to float down the river. These plus other experiences outdoors, not limited to, fishing is something I truly appreciate. I was fortunate.

Today, the value of outdoors and nature is extended to children who don't get the chance to do what I did by organizations like the **Fresh Air Fund**, serving Newark children.

65. <u>Open the door if it wasn't held for you.</u>

The effort to sacrifice and do for others even if you might not get through the door is the heroic spirit of the pioneer.

Shirley Chisolm's run to become the first black woman for President of USA in 1972 and **Jesse Jackson's** 1984 Presidential Race, opened up the idea that it might eventually be possible for the USA to elect a black person as president. Many thought it was impossible, for either of them to achieve this goal, but nevertheless, their role of planting the seed of possibility may have been enough of an effort to open the door for our current **President Barack Obama**.

66. <u>Patience and perseverance to reach personal goals is required.</u>

"A dream doesn't become reality through magic; it takes sweat, determination, and hard work".

These are the words of the **65th Secretary of State of United States, Four-Star General –General Colin Powell**.

My father would agree with this measure of what it takes to reach personal goals.

Colin Powell is an American Hero that tells it, *like it is*, just like my father. We have to encourage our children to apply this lesson if we want them to be successful.

67. Pick your head up.

When you have been rejected for a position that you desire, this is not the time to put your head down for too long.

Motivational Speaker Les Brown and my father have something in common. Even when they were rejected for a job, they learned how to pick their heads up and give it another try. Their determination, actually help them to get the kinds of jobs that many in their respective industries only dream about. I learned to do the same, every morning I would call and get rejected by about fifteen different schools as I looked for one school to hire me as a substitute teacher, until one of the school clerks said, "Yes".

Never let your head stay down too long. Align yourself with those that will help you turn a no to a yes.

68. Play a board game with your child.

This is an incredible way to bond with your child.

When a child is feeling left out, a board game can create an opportunity to let them have fun, and while you are playing the game, you can infuse valuable life lessons into the game, like some of the ones in this book.

You don't' have to agree with the examples supporting the lesson but you can still generate a dialog with the child. In many cases, the child will be able to craft new and better examples to support or reject the theory.

Playing a game can also relieve stress for you and the family.

69. Pre judging someone based on race is un-American and immoral.

After the September 11th, 2001 attacks, Muslims women were targeted on the streets of America, they were attacked and blamed for something they had nothing to do with. Ignorant people thought it was convenient to pre-judge all Muslims Arabs and those that looked like them as terrorist. The problem with this notion is that, most of the Muslim Arabs, living in the USA, had nothing to do with the attack, in fact, they themselves condemned the attack. Hopefully more Americans will look beyond race when working with humanity.

When I look at the media portrayal of people of color and study the patterns of arrests, I see a negative trend. There still seems to be the existence of racial profiling. If this is the case, then the opposite must be true, that some individuals are getting a pass, or at least getting overlooked, allowing them more freedom to conduct unethical behaviors, this is wrong.

70. <u>Pull your pants up.</u>

I think it is wrong to have your underwear showing for the public to see. I did not always think this way, according to my father. He was always telling me to wear a belt. Sometimes I forgot. Eventually, I learned the hard way. I always seemed to work slower without the belt. So dad gave me less money on pay day, I should not have to have learned like this.

Years later, I saw a young man walk into a well-known retail establishment with jeans hanging very low; then he asked the clerk if he could submit his job application; which he pulled out of his back pocket.

I wish he would have got the job, but I don't think submitting a folded up job application while your pants are sagging is a good look. Maybe add a shirt and tie, and asking to speak to the manager, will give him a better shot.

71. <u>Put your child first.</u>

Your child is your most valuable asset. Are we making sure they are developing wholesomely?

I know of parents that make sure their children are getting the training they need to succeed in life. Parents will spend thousands of dollars to give their child the edge. You don't have to spend this amount of money to give your child the edge in life. I recommend every parent place their child in extra and co-curricular activities that are free in the school system or at a low to moderate cost at other venues. Sports, speech and debate, music, dance and performance, karate or other disciplines are great options to help your child be well-rounded.

But you really don't have to pull out the checkbook. You can just spend quality time with your children. There are a lot of free events going on all the time that can make each week spectacular and enjoyable.

72. Questions can offer insights about your child.

Questions are incredible instruments parents can use to: clarify issues, open discussions, learn something new, or to help the child to express him/ herself.

My father had a series of questions he would ask to help him understand the truth. Some of the questions seem pretty intrusive. Some might say, "the issues he is questioning is too personal", he would say, "that if we are family we should be able to be personal".

At the end of the day, if you don't ask, you may never learn about the issues facing your child. You owe it to the child and yourself to ask.

73. <u>Read between the lines.</u>

Sometimes we can talk to one another but we are not really communicating. We can hear someone say that they are ok, but are we looking at other clues to determine if they are ok.

Parents, educators, social workers, and coaches have to be sensitive to the clues that are evident that don't match what the child is communicating when he says that he is ok. I always wonder about cases like the Penn State scandal. Were there adults that were close enough to the abused child to notice the signs of abuse?

Are we able to, 'read between the lines', for similar types of abuse in children of the future?

Are there behaviors that children can be taught that will make them less vulnerable to pedophiles? And are there better behaviors that professionals can adopt to minimize abuse to our children?

74. <u>Reject unsubstantiated rumors.</u>

Rumors are expressions in the media that can ruin great leaders, but amongst children, it can be socially horrifying.

Children may have difficulty navigating through the cruelty of rumors and gossip, so it is important for us to teach our children to have the internal fortitude to deflect rumors. Also we have to teach them to not to participate in the circulation of rumors.

I was encouraged by my dad to, "let rumors and gossip run off my back, like water on a duck's back".

75. <u>Religion differences must not be the barrier that divides us.</u>

The major religions of the world have more attributes in common to heal the world than they do differences, so why are we allowing extremists who misinterpret religion dictate how we must be divided?

The minister claiming to love Jesus Christ and burning or threating to burn pages from the Holy Quran represented a perverted and false reality of what Christianity is about. The persons that committed attacks on the churches in Nigeria, in the name of Islam, represent a corrupt version of what it means to be Muslim.

As a spiritual person myself, I loathe having to even mentioning these degenerate examples of humanity, but I do it to highlight the point that, **"it is up to us to showcase the best of our faiths"**

and we must sanction or admonish individuals that perform cowardly and ungodly acts in the name of promoting the faith.

Some of my strongest allies in promoting the human values I express in this book are people in almost every faith. How small-minded of me it would be, if I were to ignore their experiences.

76. <u>Rest and recreation are critical keys to rejuvenate body, mind and soul.</u>

Many workers trade rest and recreation, for longer hours of work; some people even think of it as a **"badge of honor"** to **"burn the midnight oil"**. This is a mistake.

Stress is perhaps the largest root cause of sickness in the United States of America.

One major source of stress is from overworking on the job, this means there is less time for sleep. Rest/ sleep, is a known behavior needed for recovery from illnesses and to have optimum performance on standardized tests.

Sure, there are times where we have to put in extended hours to "make ends meet" or to meet a financial goal, but we choose to sacrifice other things to do it. To save time, because we have less of it, we have to, eat more fast food, which is a less-healthier option for you to make.

This behavior leads to; increased sickness, and usually less time with family, because you are "on-the-go" too much.

Whether it is golfing, watching the football game or playing a game of chess, the time you make during the week for yourself to do something you enjoy, is effective to re-creating your energy and spirit.

Make time for yourself to get proper rest and recreation, you will be better off for it.

77. <u>SAFETY FIRST.</u>

Many of the accidents on the job, during recreation, on the streets, and around the home are very avoidable, just by making safety your number one priority.

Here are a few to think about: Simply buckling your seatbelt can save lives and minimize the severity of injury in a car accident; just ask former **NJ Governor Jon Corzine**. Wearing safety goggles is critical when handling construction equipment; especially saws that cuts wood or metal. Double checking the ropes used to tie down the furniture on top of your car before driving away from **IKEA** is a smart thing to do.

Making the effort to ensure smoke detectors are working properly, does saves lives. Taking care to not break laws like speeding or cellphone use while driving, especially in residential and business areas, demonstrates that you keep safety first, and goes a long way towards making the community a better place.

If more people and businesses prioritized safety I think we will minimize accidental claims and this will create a justification to lower the cost of accidental liability insurance. For children, we can start by making sure they wear a helmet when they ride their bikes and skateboards.

78. <u>Sacrifice is necessary to get what you want.</u>

While going to college I found it hard to get my studies completed while working two jobs. What I came to realize is that, if I did not dedicate more time to my studies I will fail my courses, or at the very least, pass them with a "C" average. This was unacceptable, because I knew one day that a "C" average would not be accepted by the NJ Department of Education for new teachers.

The sacrifice I made was to give up one of my jobs. This was a good decision, because after I did quit the job, my grades went up high enough to get on the Dean's List at Essex County College.

The moral of the story is simple; if you are not willing to give up something, to get what you want, you are not ready to acquire what you perceive you want.

79. <u>Save some of your $$$ for the future.</u>

A rainy day fund is important so that you can have a reserve in case of emergencies.

Businesses that don't spend all of their profits, but use the profits to create a reserve of funds, can bounce back when catastrophe strikes. The **BP Oil disaster of 2010** wiped out many businesses that had no reserves and insurances. Even though BP paid out many claims, some businesses could not survive long enough to have their doors open when claims were settled. This is a sad commentary for those restaurants and businesses, but we can cross-apply this to our own lives and start saving a little bit today.

Pay yourself first, and you will never be broke.

80. Security mindedness is smart.

We live in a society where some individuals have no regard for the life, liberty, or the property of others. It is necessary for us to do what we have to do in securing what is valuable to us. Locks for our bikes, burglar alarms for our homes and businesses, visible security guards in the shopping malls all are techniques to deter crime.

When children travel down the street, many are travelling with their ears flooded with music, and sometimes with hoods covering their peripheral vision. They will have jewelry, I-pads, cellphones and other electronics visible to others. To make matters worse, they may be totally engrossed in the interaction with their electronic device. All of this makes them easy targets for criminals. There is no city that has a monopoly on crime but, NYC and Newark seem to have a pattern of this in the news.

Let us do our part to minimize crime by teaching our children to be more alert when they travel.

81. Seek solace with your family.

Peace and tranquility are priceless aspects of life that everyone should be entitled to. However the reality is that these lofty goals of peace are very hard to obtain for the most of us without thoughtful planning.

Finding peace at home with family is more important than securing it at work, because home is where your family is, and they will be a part of you, for the rest of your life.

We should recognize that every child might not be able to obtain a level of peace and solace in the home. Perhaps the parents/ guardians have struggles with this topic because they have to work so much, and therefore can't create a peaceful learning environment for the child.

Perhaps there is some other issue like addiction or abuse that makes solace and peace impossible. Hopefully, there is someone in the child, and the family's life, that will assist in creating a little more peace.

If we know of children in need of solace in the home, we should make every effort to get the resources to the family and the children. Too many programs are created to reach and help only the child, but if there are no lifelines available to keep her family intact, are we doing the best justice for the child?

82. Spend time with your children.

The child is the greatest investment we can have.

Some children don't have both parents present in their lives; this is where we need to see uncles, aunts, older brothers, older sisters, and grand-parents interacting more with the child. A trip to the library, the bank, a clothing store, the supermarket, or a place of worship can go a long way towards teaching the child proper etiquette in public; and it gives the child a real first-hand account of how adults navigate in their day-to-day dealings.

This investment, gives the child a realistic perspective about life that goes beyond the limited home to school and then back home experience.

83. <u>Speak up for yourself or find someone who will.</u>

In life, there are no guarantees that adults will advocate fully for the interests of your child; therefore we must teach our children to either speak up for themselves, or to be able to identify adults that are more likely to do so.

It really boils down to this: people doing their job effectively, but sometimes people are unable to fully do their job and perhaps they may overlook your child and then your child misses out on opportunities that other children might get. Although the ASCA **(American School Counselor Association)** recommends that there are 250 students per school counselor; the national average was 459 students per school counselor, in the 2009-2010 school year. See <u>www.asca.org</u>

If there was a scholarship opportunity, college application to complete, SAT voucher to receive, or college tour to participate in, would your child miss out? Or are we discussing these issues with our children to make sure they are engaged with the guidance office at their school.

I remember my father telling me a story about when a school counselor dismissed his aspiration of becoming an environmental engineer. Sometimes, I wonder how his life path would have been different, if the counselor had the time to guide him, or if someone was available to challenge the dismissal by the counselor of his aspirations. We will never know, but you can teach your child how to deal with this by teaching her to speak up for herself, and encouraging her to cross-check all adult conversations with the parent.

84. <u>Sports can foster discipline and other benefits.</u>

You can ask the child, how they might benefit from being on a sports team. There are too many benefits to list here.

Few experiences in a child's K-12 educational experience can have a larger influence on his/ or her life than engagement in a consistent activity beyond the classroom.

When I mention sports can foster discipline such as track, baseball, wrestling, basketball or football; it could just as well be debate, speech, drama, karate, chorus, the band, cheerleading, Stand & Deliver, Close Up, the Chess Club, the National Honor Society, or the Math Club. All of these experiences can usher in the kinds of benefits we want for your child.

The coaches of the team can serve as mentors for the child, while advocating for the child on the other fronts that may be neglected by the school or at home.

Plus the members of the team can serve an extended family pushing the child to do more. The discipline to the particular activity is acquired as the child continues to do the drills, exercises and work required to be a part of competition, and the skills learned in the activity, can be utilized in other aspects of a child's life.

85. <u>Sportsmanship and respect go hand-in-hand.</u>

Few things are worse to see than bad attitudes: before, during, and after competition between children.

We can work with coaches to ensure that our children are honorable, that they shake hands after the match, and that the child is doing everything they can do, to be competitive. Sore losers have not learned how to do it gracefully, and while working with his/ her home team they might acquire this skill. Respect for themselves, the team, the sport equipment, the school grounds, and the competitor, in time, will be evident as the child remains under the instruction of a good coach.

One high school coach, expecting his team players to be model leaders in the school, overheard one of the players cursing and disrespecting an adult faculty member. He immediately, stopped the squad, and yelled this order to the young man, **"Take that jersey off, you no longer represent the team!"** This sent a clear message, to all the other players that you can't be disrespectful to others and expect to play, even if you are my star player.

Respect and good sportsmanship can be obtained in all of our schools.

86. <u>Stand up for what you believe in.</u>

People will not know your position, if you do NOT stand up for your principles and beliefs.

I saw my father stand up to all sorts of people.

From immature eyes, I thought he was crazy, but from more mature eyes, I concluded, who else would stand up for the common worker on the various construction sites if he did not.

There has to be individuals and groups that stand up for the right issues; which is why I have admiration for the **Occupy Movements** that are publicizing concerns for themselves and for those that are unable or unwilling to speak for themselves.

Would you change your mind if your superiors pressured you to do something that goes against your beliefs? Not if you were **Paul Robeson**. This all-around Renaissance man and humanitarian who spoke over 25 different languages, was extraordinarily talented in academics, sports, acting, legal studies, singing, and much more. Every child should do research on Paul Robeson before they graduate.

During the age of Jim Crow segregation in the USA, this African-American would attract thousands of people to watch his performances. However, if he came to the stage to perform and saw the crowd segregated, in other words where the black people were sitting behind the white people, he would refuse to perform. This action by Robeson would infuriate his promoters, but he stood his ground. If we teach our children about real examples like him, perhaps they will learn that it is possible to stand on your principles and excel.

87. Team work makes the dream work.

Individually we can accomplish a lot, but as a team we can do much more.

Think about all the extreme success of **Serena and Venus Williams**. It was the combined team of them, under the direction of their father **Richard Williams** that moved the game of tennis to a new era. If you study the dynamics of the relationship within the team you will realize that it is because, the daughters were on the same page as the father, they were able to be successful. The same is true, of the dynamics that existed between Tiger Woods and his Father.

Being on the same page ideological and in practice equates to being on the same team, and we can do so much more.

88. <u>Think before you speak.</u>

Frequently, we hear political leaders saying things that, just does not make sense. Or they will say things that are so insensitive that to say they are politically incorrect might be candy coating the issue.

Politicians thoughtless statements serve as insults and bully antics to the listening audience, and I think if they would have thought about the question raised before speaking, a more appropriate response would have been given.

Some of the political debates we are hearing in the news are loaded with slick negative personal comments that have little to do with the concerns of the constituents. Perhaps these political leaders could have learned a lesson or two about respect, civility and good sportsmanship from the coach featured in the last lesson.

The fast pace of today's media encourages us to speak quickly, but if there is no thought behind it, then it is nothing but a lot of hot gas. Think before you speak.

89. <u>Think outside of the box.</u>

If you do things the way everybody else does them, then you will confine yourself to the status quo of everyone else.

What I learned about my father's actions is that he would take the typical foundation of knowledge that we study and he would cross-apply it to situations that does not normally apply to that train of thought, similar to **George Washington Carver**. George Washington Carver was such a brilliant, "out of the box" thinker that he invented 300 different applications of the simple peanut plant.

Professor Carver was able to successfully think out of the box, and therefore more able to help many farmers to profit year round from their land instead of just the fall harvest; in his book called, **"Help for Hard Times"**.

Out of the box thinkers are not afraid to do the uncommon, especially if it is for a noble cause.

90. TRUST but keep your eyes open.

There is an expression in some communities that says it best, "Trust in God but tie your camel".

Unbeknownst to me, my dad made a commitment to keep eyes on me as I rode my bicycle in those far away neighborhoods that we worked in. He knew the history of boys disappearing in the South and was not leaving my journey and play to chance. He also taught me to not leave my open drinks and my food around where guys on the job could readily tamper with it. This is a lesson some should use when they have exposed food and drinks at house parties.

We also learned to take care of securing our work tools each and every night. Crew members who were careless in securing their walking stilts (worth a couple of hundred dollars) could not complete their ceiling work the following morning if they were stolen.

We can have trust in people, but we must secure and monitor the things we cherish.

91. Turn off the Television aka "Tell-Lie-Vision".

Television is loaded with fictional fun and entertainment, but because the programing was not based in reality; it seems to be a waste of valuable time. One study printed on the **California State University website** says that, **"the average American spends 4 hours a day watching television"**. It goes on to say, "This works out to be 9 years out of a 65 year old life span". You can almost earn a doctor degree in that amount of time.

My father believed this, and worked hard to make sure our exposure to television was controlled as best he could. I was fascinated by *"Knight Rider"* and the 'good ole boys' of the *"Dukes of Hazard"* and many other shows. Now that I think about it; too much television seemed to have erased some of my creative energy.

Network producers paid anywhere between 1 to 2 million dollars per episode for the hit television sitcom series called

"Family Matters". The most significant message that I found for me after laughing at the jokes was that it was more important for me to get rid of my eye glasses, to look cool, "to get the girls". And the next most important message is that I as black boy absorbed, from this sitcom, is that the **_smart school nerd_** had zero chance, of getting the girl of his dreams.

Every parent should try to know what their children watch, so that there could be a discussion.

92. <u>Unwanted by society still welcome by us.</u>

Somewhere on the **Statute of Liberty** it says, **"give us your tired and poor"**, this should be the spirit of the institutions in my community and those that set up businesses here.

It was sad to see how general contractors would build large communities in Newark, like Society Hills and other developments, but there would rarely be decent money when they had to pay the immigrants and the blacks. Prevailing wage was supposed to ensure decent hourly wages for professionals but I guess there were no inspectors to check. "This is the pay, take it or leave it!", is what they would say to my dad. And he would fight for the better wage. My dad would take those guys that could not find jobs in other places, train them in the art of 'finishing' and he was proud to give them a decent salary.

My dad was committed to the idea of helping his people, and at one point he employed as many as thirty men at the same time. I think the men and the contractors respected my father's commitment to this ideal.

93. U-turns are allowed by the Creator.

Too often people make it their business to judge and predict the final outcome of others. They make assumptions that some people can't achieve a particular goal in life.

If a person has a past that is less than desirable, it is not up to me to be the final determinant of her destiny, and even if, I make a negative judgment about someone, it does not and should not determine his/ her fate. Let the individual be focused, and determined to improve himself, and prove my decision wrong.

At the end of the day, it is not people that will help you turn your life around; it is only your relationship and commitment to something higher than man; which affords you an opportunity to turnaround.

94. <u>Victory by the children is our victory.</u>

I believe that every parent's natural inclination is to see their children be successful.

With that being said, the child that is unruly may have forgotten the nature and purpose of the parent. If the child understands this concept, then the parent and child are said to be on the same page. The child that does not appreciate the efforts of the parent is not likely to put the best foot forward in being victorious at much of anything.

Encourage your child to count their blessings, and to use those gifts to gain success.

95. **Volunteer for an organization you value.**

Volunteering is another aspect to life that creates a greater sense of purpose.

One to two hours once a week, can begin to get you acquainted with giving back to the community, or start your pathway to an internship for a career beyond high school/ college.

The volunteer "candy stripping" at a young age in U.M.D.N.J. hospital, helped me to get a better understanding of a hospital's pharmaceutical department inner workings. It was time well served.

96. <u>Voting comes, then politicians must serve the people.</u>

Sometime the leaders in office need to be reminded that their job is to serve the people.

Contractors on construction jobs would get away with as much as they could legally and illegally, and it was my father who believed that politicians had a duty to protect the interest of their constituents. What a novel idea!

Dad would call on politicians to put pressure on contractors managing large development sites that were not paying the workers for weeks at a time.

Sadly, some of the politicians he contacted would not see this as a priority, but he has not lost faith in the system, and I have not either. The political climate of 2012 requires all of us to put pressure on every politician that wishes to serve us, and ask then to do even more.

If your child has aspirations to go into politics encourage them to do some internships with City Hall or the school board. If your child is old enough, they should register to vote.

It doesn't matter which political party they affiliate with, as long as we can vote, we will begin to hold leaders more accountable to do the right thing.

97. <u>Walk away before resorting to terrible acts.</u>

The pressure or comfort that may come from being in a group might make a child be tempted to do many things, even if those things are wrong and illegal. If you can consult with the right adult about the challenges and experiences you face, then it might be possible to preempt the dilemma before it occurs. If your intuition tells you that your friends are about to do a wrong act, you don't have to participate. Distance yourself before the problem escalates.

98. Work smart and work hard.

When you are building yourself worth, you have to be committed to both – working hard and smart.

Some of the young people are under the impression that they can succeed by just adopting one or the other idea in relationship to getting ahead. This is a fallacy and perversion of reality that they may have learned off of one of the *"tell-lie-vision"* sitcoms, or perhaps they adopted the whispering suggestions heard on the radio. In both cases, the media suggests that if you work hard you will get to the top; or it will show you that if you are smart, you can rise rapidly to the top.

In all of the real life examples that I studied, there was always some combination of hard and smart work that made them stand out, to be successful.

99. <u>You are the best.</u>

It is a simple expression that can lift the spirits of a child when a parent thinks they need it.

My father perhaps one of my biggest constructive critics in adult life, had a way of making me feel special as I grew up, even though I knew my actions was less than stellar.

Him telling me that, "You are the best", helped to carry me through moments that were less than successful in my youth.

With children, I think we have to constantly find ways and activities that can help them highlight attributes that make them the best or special. At the end of the day, it will be worth the effort.

At: Right: Steve Jobs holds the popular Apple iPad. (Wikimedia Commons)

100. Zeal for a wholesome life --- every moment, is what we should strive for. This is perhaps the most important concept to teach and pass on to others. I think that we must teach our children to cherish every moment. I believe my dad tried to instill this in me. At a 2005 Stanford University Commencement Address, **Steve Jobs**, the iconic visionary of the technological savvy Apple Computers once said, *"Your time is limited, so don't waste it living someone else's life. Don't be trapped by dogma - which is living with the results of other people's thinking. Don't let the noise of other's opinions drown out your own inner voice. And most important, have the courage to follow your heart and intuition. They somehow already know what you truly want to become. Everything else is secondary."* I agree.

One of the most well-known international humanitarians, philanthropists, and champions of this era, **Muhammad Ali** once said, *"He who is not courageous enough to take risks will accomplish nothing in life".* Muhammad Ali is a hero with the courage that has embodied almost all of the humble lessons I put forth in this book. He sacrificed things he loved most, as he stood up against segregation, the military draft and all forms of inequality, historic and contemporary. Ali is a champion in every sense of the word, and an example of what it means to have a zealous and wholesome life. Every student should be required to learn about Muhammad Ali, so that perhaps they will understand why he was often called, "The Greatest", then selected by Sports Illustrated as "The Sportsman of the Century", and "Sports Personality of the Century" by the BBC. If we could have the zeal of ALI, we can change the world for the better.

About the Author:

Educational Leader- Tariq T. Raheem, is a Social Studies teacher for over 14 years in Newark, New Jersey. He has founded a nationally-competitive high school policy debate team and has served as its coach for ten years. Then he elected to be the senior teacher crafting the 2008 Newark Public Schools Debate Curriculum Addendum.

Earning a Master of Arts Degree in Education Administration and passing the Principal Certification Test for the State of New Jersey, only reaffirmed Mr. Raheem's, commitment to be a lifelong educator. His studies through the supervisory course work, and his past commitment to the National Network of Pathways Scholars has given him insight to see many of the challenges plaguing the educational systems in cities across America. During his journey, he has been able to determine what works to help every student win, regardless of ability or background.

Mr. Raheem believes that every child deserves to have all the resources they need to help them reach their destination, and if those resources are not available in the school and/or home life then the child is lost. He believes there are tangible options for administrators and parents, that are free or of low-cost, which can improve a young person's life. He has a passion and love for using civil discourse as a method to reach and teach children.

Equally as important for him as his public school service, Mr. Raheem enjoys piloting creative learning experiences not limited to the classroom. In his quest to prepare students for leadership he has engaged his students in: We The People Competition, Close Up-Washington D.C , Student Voices, NJ State Bar Foundation Mock Trials, Essex County Law Day, Rutgers Minority Recruitment Law Day, numerous other Civic Fairs district-wide, and several models of debate in the National Forensics League. He is proud to have his students featured on C-Span2 TV-"Newseum", ABC TV, BET Television, WBGO Radio, NY Times, the Star-Ledger, and more.

Tariq T. Raheem has presented at conventions & workshops, and published works to promote his values on improving education to help the child. Here is a partial list:

1. **Improving and Moving .com** www.improvingandmoving.com (current website)
2. *"Can We Improve Our Child's Ability to Succeed in This Sacred Life?"* at the Annual National Muslim American Society Convention- September 2010
3. *"Was the July 4, 1176 Signing of the Declaration of Independence Sparked by the Desire of African-Americans to Escape Slavery?"* Improving Education Blog- 2010
4. Law Day Mock Trial (led by students) ITV to students from Tennessee to Canada- 2010
5. *"8 Dynamic Ways to Usher in Success"* -2010
6. *"Can Children Be Taught Important Life Lessons Through Board Games?"* -2010
7. *"3 Solid Ways to Improve Education in All Schools Through Your PTA"* -2010
8. *"5 Easy and Enduring Memorial Lessons All Parents Can Teach Their Children"* -2010
9. *"We Must Teach and Respect Diversity for Every Student"* -2010
10. *"A Primer on How to Improve Education"* -2010
11. *"O Say Can We See?"*Student-driven Historical Research Task for Project Fair – 2010
12. *"The History of African-American Women in the Christian Ministry"* -2009
13. *"Year 2010 Re-Solved"* (a campaign to realign your life for the better) -2009
14. *"Learn What It Takes to Reverse The Trend of Low Performing Schools"*-2009
15. *"Simple Strategies to Reduce Drop Out Rates in Public Schools"* -2009
16. *"Your 2010 Resolutions: Re- Solved and Resolved- We Cannot Stop Now!"* -2009
17. *"$10,000 of Your Money Back in Your Pocket"* - How To Do It - 2009

18. Improving and Moving -Print Edition – December 2009
19. *"How To Be a Successful Policy Debate Coach"* for Jersey Urban Debate League-2008
20. *"A Piece of History Every American Should Know"* Student Project Fair - 2009 and 2008
21. *"Strategies and Opportunities for Students to Speak Out"* National Convention – 2006
22. *"How To Be a Better Parent"*- Pathway National Teacher Convention Philadelphia-2005
23. *"The Direction of Clara Muhammad Schools Nationwide"* - 2004
24. Monthly Lectures to community members on topics of (education, religion, history, motivation, business development, etc...) from 1996-2005 over 100 lecturers on audio

Tariq T. Raheem can be contacted for educational consultation, motivational/ informational lectures, staff development, workshops etc... via Email at: coachraheem@gmail.com